I0159968

Tasting Flight

poems

Praise for *Tasting Flight*:

The poems in this collection are confidently crafted, spiritually and emotionally insightful and precise, and intelligent all at once. Rosenfeld does not shy away from the hardest subject matter and makes language equal to it. "On Becoming a Woman," a moving and surprising mother/daughter poem, is the best I've read on this subject. Rooted in the origin myths of Genesis when the Divine "stepped out of itself onto the slick, dark lid of otherness," *Tasting Flight* unflinchingly questions, complicates, and celebrates what it means to be a woman and to be deeply, imperfectly, human.

—Joy Ladin, National Jewish Book Award-winning author of
The Book of Anna and *Shekhinah Speaks*

Yiskah Rosenfeld's *Tasting Flight* is both a sampling of subtle variations of spirit and a winging off the ground in self-reclamation. These are strongly crafted poems, wide ranging in form and genre, steeped in the vocabulary of Jewish customs and texts in cross-cultural conversation, as when the speaker tugs and worries the fringes of a prayer shawl "like rosaries, frayed jeans." We discover the making of a self through the landscapes of cities, alphabets, stars, planets, languages, hours on the clock, and relationships, with explorations along the edges. Among myriad mysteries is the certainty that "I don't deserve" because "I am not pretty" and identifications with the desires of Eve and the skin of Miriam until in a culminating poem, the speaker, prostrate in gratitude, finds herself "bowing to myself, big-bellied as Buddha and just as deserving." In poems dense with thought and rich in feeling, a life in its details finds vital significance in the context of long timelines and a vast, expanding universe.

—Lori Hope Lefkovitz, founding executive director of ritualwell.org
and author of *In Scripture: The First Stories of Jewish Sexual Identity*

Tasting Flight

poems

Yiskah Rosenfeld

MADVILLE
PUBLISHING

LAKE DALLAS, TEXAS

Copyright © 2024 by Yiskah Rosenfeld
All rights reserved
Printed in the United States of America

FIRST EDITION

Requests for permission to reprint or reuse material from this work
should be sent to:

Permissions
Madville Publishing
PO Box 358
Lake Dallas, TX 75065

Cover Design: Noam Rosenfeld

Cover Art: Embroidered silk from a Noh Costume, Japan.
(Nuihaku) with Egret (Sagi) and Willow Tree.
Edo period (1615–1868). Museum of Modern Art, New York.

Author Photo: Cheshire Isaacs

ISBN: 978-1-956440-83-6 paperback
978-1-956440-84-3 ebook
Library of Congress Control Number: 2024933886

For Noam, who teaches me daily how to be her mother

We bear the seeds of our return forever,
The flowers of our leaving, fruit of flight

—Muriel Rukeyser, *Theory of Flight*

Contents

1   Origins

WHAT YOU CALL FALLING

5   To Whom It May Concern

7   Brown-Headed Cowbirds

8   Café Leila After Lockdown

10   Eve's Confession

12   Bird Call Koan with Glossary

17   Saving Daylight

18   Little Girl Blue

20   Ciphers and Constellations

23   *Klippot*

24   Naamah

26   Driving My Mother to Acupuncture

28   The States that Made Me

29   A Lesson in Fractions

31   Shooting the Square

32   *Tashlich*

33   *Untitled* 1954/55

35   On Becoming a Woman

37   The Apple Tree and the Fig Tree

ALIGHT

41   Hamsah

43   Safety Matches

45   *Yehi Or* (And There Was Light)

47   Inside the Room, Outside the Night

49   A Question of Night

52   My Father's Study

54   California Oak Moths

55   Arterials

56   *Havdalah*

57   Entrance to the Letter *Aleph*

58   Cardamom and Myrrh

59   Inside the *Genizah*

60   Two Dreams at Beth-El

61   Rio Caliente

62   Notturno in D

64   Miriam's Skin

65   Sonnet for Habib Koité

66   Questions for My Tibetan Healer

67   Bath and Afterbath

69   Summoning the *Shechinah*

NOBODY'S APPLE

73   Late Afternoon at Café Roma

74   Twilight's Poem, Dawn-Written

77   7 a.m. at the Western Wall

78   All These Gaps

79   Mud Soup

81   Perfect Paring

84   New Moon of the Month of *Nissan*

85   Meridian

86   A Woman Asks to Be Named

88   Desert Is a Mouth Opening

89   *Techelet*

90   Learning the Essentials

93   Birdwatcher

94   The Morning After a Vipassana Retreat

95   Seventh Day in the Valley

96   Alone on My Daughter's First Night of Sleepaway Camp

99   *Tishre*

100   Notes

102   Acknowledgments

105   About the Author

Origins

Flight

God said, "It is not good for Adam to be alone" (Genesis 2:18). So God made him a woman from the earth like him, and called her Lilith. They immediately began arguing: She said, "I will not lie below." And he said, "I will not lie below, but above, since you are fit for being below and I for being above." She said, "The two of us are equal, since we are both from the earth." Because Lilith saw how it was, she uttered the ineffable name and flew away into the air. God sent three angels after her to bring her back, but she would not return.

—*The Alphabet of Ben Sira*, c. 8th-10th century

Taste

When the woman saw that the fruit of the tree was good to eat and a delight to the eye, and the tree was desirable for wisdom, she took of its fruit and ate (Genesis 3:6).

What fruit did Eve give Adam? Rabbi Meir said, "It was grapes, because nothing makes one wail more than wine." Rabbi Nehemiah said, "It was figs; that which caused their downfall, rectified it. As it is written, 'And they took fig leaves and made for themselves coverings' (Genesis 3:7)." Rabbi Yehuda said, "It was wheat, since an infant only knows how to call mother and father after tasting grain."

—the Babylonian Talmud

What You Call Falling

Desire is hunger is the fire I breathe
Love is a banquet on which we feed

—"Because the Night," Patti Smith
and Bruce Springsteen

To Whom It May Concern

I am writing to let you know that I am not
too ugly to be a poet. Thank you for your concern.

You say old men can be poets but not old women.
You say old men can be gods but not old women.

Thank you for this drawer of letters
stashed in my heart on which you have written

I can't be a poet because I am too ugly.
I can't be a gardener because I am too ugly.

I can't dance freely in white through the fields
in joy because I am too ugly.

Everyone is allowed, you say, but if you are ugly,
it's best to stay home.

You say I can cry in dark corners.
You say I can curl in my bed like a crustacean.

You say it is perfectly okay to be ugly on the bus,
in my house, at Target. I can be ugly at night.

There are so many things I can do and be ugly.
I should not be discouraged. We can't all be hummingbirds.

Thank you for advice so generously given.
But I must inform you that the garden itself

is ugly, the damp clods of dirt I rake with my fingers,
worms coming up writhing their pink S bodies,

and the misshapen pebbles. I can kneel down
in the mulch and be with who they are.

Also, the dark thoughts that feed my poems,
those inking this very paper in bursts of octopus fury,

are ugly: hard pellets sometimes, smashed summer fruit,
bloody, fat-marbled steaks, crumbs born of crumbs.

I can stir myself into that soup.
You are welcome to taste.

Brown-Headed Cowbirds

My child fits the ball of the earth in her palm.
I can't. Can't squeeze it all into one blue fistful,
stroke its cheek and mother it the way it needs.

I am giving it up for adoption,
like the cowbirds who lay their eggs
in little songbirds' nests.

When they hatch, the songbird mother wears herself out
keeping those big cowbird chicks alive.
All she knows: to feed any open mouth.

Soft throat of the world,
I won't be feeding you anymore.
Are there enough words left to fill you up?

Let the nest of my hands
clasp the mountain and the hunger
to its makeshift ribs.

Café Leila After Lockdown

Head hidden by leaves, six gold arms,
elbows folding in, elbows folding out,
hand floating gently over chest
like a shield to protect the heart.

Whatever moves, whatever moves—
water cascading the rusted fountain,
birds swinging down and gone,
the giddy voices of friends who have not

touched or hugged in 15 months,
passing glazed ceramic bowls around in wonder,
the plate of sun-sized pancakes tilted
in the upraised hand of the server,

someone sliding their chair into shade,
how her hips swerve between tables,
the few leaves barely lifting at the top
of the overgrown ivy, and again at the top

of the date palm, and again, higher, at the top
of the overgrown oak tree which conceals
the face, the breeze rippling
the surface of Genmaicha tea—

is measured against that still gilt hand,
center of this morning's universe.
And what do my hands measure? They hold,
in sequence, a pen, a triangle

of seeded watermelon, the curve of a teacup,
an iPhone with its calculated width and weight.
The pattern repeats: pen, wedge, cup, phone,
pen, wedge, cup, phone, the blank glass

dissolving to color when lifted
like the queen's magic mirror.
This time I raise an empty hand instead.
Unmasked, skirt tables, dip

under thick branches to find
not one face, but three. Lord Vishnu.
One hand makes an O, the others hold
a shell, a book, a wheel, a jar.

The language at the tables I pass
skips like herons skimming water for food,
lilts and lands lightly. Tibetan, turning
even English into tinkling bells.

If he opened his book, would this language
flap suddenly and fly out?
Vishnu keeps it sealed shut.
That hand does not move from his heart.

We, in our opposite corners, hold down this day,
like heavy bowls pinning a tablecloth.
Even so, there is nothing in this garden
that can't take flight.

Eve's Confession

As if I could speak
having been given no language
only desire

        wanting only
        the power
        to name what I want.

                I was born from the side
                and this is how I entered all rooms:
                shuffling, apologetic, peripheral.

        Without a center
        I quickly learned
        how circles work

how they steer you
around the core of things
clinging to peripheries

        how easy it is
        to hide
        so far from beginnings

                and always arriving at the same place
                only more full, flustered
                heavy with secrets and a thin film

        of darkness
        which, I also learned,
        is not the same as sin.

It was his shape that drew me
round in body and logic
our thoughts encircling—

A question of dialogue
not commandment.
Don't judge me:

>   What you call falling
>   was the closest I've come
>   to pure statement.

I brought us into the world
out of desire,
not language

and it was worth the risk:
After the garden
I bore our son

>   from the center of my self
>   I bore our son
>   and I named him.

Bird Call Koan with Glossary

in memory of Dr. Ibrahim Farajajé

TOOLOOL, TOOLOOL
> *What if I were beautiful, what if I were enough?*

TOOLOOL, TOOLOOL
> *What if I were beautiful, what if I were enough?*

My child whispers that when the moon is a crescent, she can see the shape of the whole outlined black against the blue-black sky. I tell her there's a side of the moon we never see. She lies in the dark contemplating this, cycling her Fisher-Price lullabies over and over into the night.

Across the hall I lie in the dark contemplating this, the infinitely expanding universe of what I don't know. Stars exploding and being born. Moons in our own solar system still uncounted. And yet some things I think I know with certainty: I'm not pretty. I don't deserve to be loved.

If I trill my mating call, who will answer me?

I forget the moon is always whole.

WHEEDELEE, KUEU KUEU KUEU
>*What if I were less than the fluff of milkweed,*
>*greater than the Milky Way?*

WHEEDELEE, KUEU KUEU KUEU
>*What if I were less than the fluff of milkweed,*
>*greater than the Milky Way?*

>Ibrahim Baba, when you were in a coma I prayed this prayer: Don't let too much love and too much suffering burst your heart. But once you tasted death, you couldn't put it down. Too tempting to escape the limitations of an ill-fitting body, the cruel politics of academia, all the places a 6'5" Black Muslim *tzitzit*-wearing orange-bearded pierced tattooed genderqueer father trying to save the world can't squeeze.

>The basket you brought, once full of apples, still waits by the door. When my father was dying you told me you were holding us in the cave of your heart. I kept the voicemail as if to capture you in it like a firefly in a jar. You were too much light.

>Now that you can skate Saturn's rings and vibrate the constellations, can you hear your son's Persian melodies on the tanbur without ears to telescope eternity into song?

Can you recite Rumi where you are if Rumi is the object of a question

about desire to be made whole?

CHICKADEEDEE, CHICKADADADEEDEEDEE
  Is anyone looking, is anyone looking for me?

CHICKADEEDEE, CHICKADADADEEDEEDEE
  Is anyone looking, is anyone looking for me?

The map of my brain realigns itself, more water between islands now.

I lie awake.   I trust the boat.   I trust the boat.

I trust the boat will come to take me back.

Experiment in drowning. Rest in cling. Drown again.

The half-moon reflects so brightly it knocks the stars out of the sky.
I feel I rose to see it, as if called.

Sometimes there's a knowing and a nothing. A know and a no.

Do we love the moon any less when it's not full?

CHIRUP CHIREEP CHIRUP
    Hush, my babies, time to sleep

CHIRUP CHIREEP CHIRUP
    Hush, my babies, time to sleep

נומי נומי ילדתי נומי נומי נים

Numi numi yaldati numi numi nim

Hush the lullabies, my chickadee.
Let me hold you.

Numi numi chemdati numi numi nim

נומי נומי חמדתי נומי נומי נים

You who taught me the moon is always whole,

    let me hold you in the nest of my heart.

GLOSSARY

TOOLOOL, TOOLOOL   Blue jay: A bell-like call of two parts, both
                             on the same pitch. Call and response
                             in courtship flocks.

WHEEDELEE KUEU KUEU KUEU   Blue jay: Given during courtship and
                             nest building.

CHICKADEEDEE   Black-capped chickadee: Given by a
CHICKADADEEDEEDEE   bird that has become separated from
                             the flock, or given after a disturbance
                             has dispersed the flock; has the effect
                             of bringing the flock back together.

CHIRUP CHIREEP CHIRUP   House sparrow: Given by the male
                             when he is perched near the nest and
                             hasn't found a mate, or the female
                             who has lost her mate.

—*A Guide to Bird Behavior*, Volume I, Donald Stokes (1979)

Saving Daylight

Then I remembered. Then I remembered not
to be awake because for an extra hour
the soft, hot body will crawl next to mine
faint smell of rocket ship innocence and pee
bright light through the curtains time
to get ready for school the way it was
time in Kansas to pull clothes
from the white dresser, toes sunk in pink carpet
hide behind the Life cereal box, find shoes
best suited to autumn leaves and smack of cool—
Don't forget your coat—but different now
because I am the mother it's 40 odd years later
more watery the California sun, he scoops
his own cereal from the clear container
with a white ¼ measuring cup
puts milk in first then too many Cheerios,
tries to pat them down with the back of a spoon.
I am not in a red velour zipped dressing gown
like my mother but might as well be
old yoga pants and oversized Hello Kitty shirt
same bare feet disheveled hair sudden flashes of anger
more frightening on this end where the tall power
to harm originates—*mothers are gods aren't we,*
we are terrible, terrible gods—I swipe
the milk up myself lean against the granite counter
getting my news from the flat screen in my hand
as if better than losing my father behind curtains
of creased newspaper. He chooses his shoes from
a basket by the door—Superman today—I let him go
without slicking his hair down not even a jacket
and then it's just me scrambling an egg, my mother's
shadow pouring coffee in the blue glazed mug
a scene out of Picasso's blue period maybe
or the original *Star Trek*, some kind of bending
of time to gaze face to face at our mid-life selves
and why not, look how easy it is to spin back
the hands of a watch. *Lonely, isn't it*, the shadow says,
emptying packets of Sweet'n Low onto the red Formica
like sands through the hourglass on *Days of Our Lives*.

Little Girl Blue

for my daughter, whom I mistook for a boy for five years

The sheep's in the meadow,
the cow's in the corn,

little boy blue sleeps
in his train and plane pajamas

long hair ratted up like a haystack,
untethered dreams

tossing and turning the world
until it's all mixed up.

Let him sleep.
Let the day unknit

from its tightly pearled
configurations

goodgirls and silverbells
lined up all in a row

plastic shapes pushed
into wooden shape absences

ninjas on one aisle, fairies the other
trapped in the wrong room,

wrong body, arranging the dots
that swim behind pressed lids.

Let her sleep.
Let the cows go wild in the fields

sheep stomp the meadows
with petals in their teeth

chair jump over the moon
lamp and the desk

splay out its legs
to rest on its wide oak belly.

Will you wake her? No, not I.
For if we do, she's sure to cry.

Ciphers and Constellations

The spectacle of the sky overwhelms me. I'm overwhelmed when
I see, in an immense sky, the crescent of the moon, or the sun.
—Joan Miró

1

The summer of making do, morning dew
tastes like Frosted Flakes in a split wide box,
manna we scrape off the leaves

blessing the cool shade
before the sun sets it all on fire.
My child wants to believe

her teeth are wiggling.
She gets the whole world rocking
to prove it.

Even the weeds are scrawny,
leaned up against the fence
like bored kids outside the liquor store.

Whatever words might name
this crackling cement melt
under the sun's relentless heat.

2

Night is something else. Out of the tent to pee.
Alone in the dark meadow to dizzy down
under a clear sky teeming with stars.

Try to pin down what I'm witnessing
and fail, turn animal instead.
Let the sky just be its dazzling self.

Crescent moon. I see a listening ear.
Forest, I'm falling apart.
Trauma keeps reinventing itself.

My child sunk down in a sleeping bag
lined with pines, in a tent under pines.
Her dreams wax and wane.

Turns out tree therapy is just to go on being trees.
Being is enough.
I write it down on paper. *Tov.* טוֹב I am good.

Big and little dippers ladle black soup back and forth.
Each star a solar system we can't see.
All the time we put into our little ones.

Not *very* good, *tov me'od,* טוֹב מְאֹד like in the Torah
when humans were created, the sixth day.
Just fair to middling good.

3

Each child a sun we orbit, an intricate galaxy
of gravitational pull we only grasp a fraction of,
to the closest moon perhaps.

Words scrawl larger and larger,
the gaps grow bigger between them
like the increasingly vast spaces between gas planets,

millions of galaxies—lenticular, elliptical, spiral—
spin like Spirographs,
swim me closer to sleep,

the last illegible scrawls
swirling and zigzagging the page
as bold and childlike as any Miró.

Later, I can just make out the words
alphabet train, measurements of failure, joy.
If even those.

Klippot

The way a snap and two chewed pistachios gave us these.
The way they resemble teeth, but husked and unmouthed.

The way I need five to make a flower but they come in pairs.
The way my child looks to me for instruction, to know why.

The way we hold them to our heads and call them ears.
The way we hold them over our eyes and call them eyes.

The random urge to paint pupils on them.
The soft fingertip rub of their backs.

The way they stay on the table for weeks, reconfiguring,
now in a row, now scattered, now stacked.

The way we are told to cast them off, our *klippot*,
but they are raincoats, they are wings,

they tell the story of the nut that was, they cradle
emptiness in their baskets as well as any mother.

Cinderella's shoe, a cap for a mouse, castanets,
my child and I quiet in their presence; we know holiness.

The way I say shell as if it were fact.
The way she says it, like a ship at sea.

Naamah

for M., a trans Palestinian who came to the U.S. seeking asylum

Two by two the words step out
of your mouth's arc
testing the dry invitation of air.
Your tongue sets out in search of peace
licks the tender under-salt of olives
returns a messenger, a god, a bird.

When home is a boat to settle is to set
sail, what feels like gentle rocking
is a slow lilt in some tidal direction
no matter how hard your palms press
no matter how still you become.

When home is a red cabin on a hill
its windows bowing in three directions
and the river stretched on her back below
like a lazy cat, you will unanchor
the glass sheeted with autumn rains
all your languages wiped clean.

One morning you will awaken,
alive, alive, go down to the river
to rest your fertile body against
the one made of light
male and female, sky and sea
Yahweh and Elohim, raven and dove—

two into one into two into one,
embraced, all, in the water's soft lullabies
feathered into one heartbeat by your hands'
joyful swift-slapping on the drum
steady and quick like the old women fashioning bread
on the side of the road to Beersheba.

Did you think you would end where you started?
Did you think it was that kind of door?
Come through, come close, come home,
kiss that complexity back to its rooted whole.
O Righteous One, *Habibi* حبيبي
you, too, walk with God.

Driving My Mother to Acupuncture

Reiko sets me
in the one chair at the back
of the house with the red door
on the street my mother
always forgets to turn onto.
Shoes line the entrance.

Books line the walls.
Japanese and English trickle their spines
while down the hall my mother
removes her wig, hair thinned
to reddish cobwebs, the scalp almost sexual
in its sudden exposure.

In the one chair in the empty room
I read the Bible, run my tongue
down the blessings and curses
and taste the old rules of childhood:
curses are caused; blessings are luck,
chance baskets arriving by wind.

Inside my mother the gift, unbidden, flowers.
Who sent it? The day warm and breezy
as if earned by good behavior,
but inside her breast, the curse,
condensed to a not-ripe fruit,
a second, smaller heart.

Reiko boils water for tea,
serves me medallions of candied ginger,
sweet rolled leaves of seaweed.
I don't know what I've done
to deserve this, the cup smaller than my hand,
tea hot and swollen with peach.

Sweetness pins the galaxy's center
to this chair, at this moment;
my mother's muted voice softly orbits.
Sugar and sour, blessing and curse,
my mouth accepts how they coexist,
how an empty room makes room in any language.

I think of the shoes
lined up at the door like obedient horses,
how whatever is stowed in our hearts,
mother, daughter, bitter, sweet,
the shoes will bear us up,
the shoes will take us
where we need to go.

The States that Made Me

New York

My mother's key
to the world, or Ohio.
Loose and bumpy like her fist
curled at her side when she walks.
Rubbing up against most Northeastern states
damp from the recurring dream of drifting,
anchorless. An immigrant with one foot
still in the boat, finger pointing
to the West.

Oregon

 Broken   crown   cast
from a mine   of Goldblums   and bergs,
risk-takers who journeyed too far to have children
who won't clean their plates. Shorter baking times,
colder hearts. Everything growing too tall too fast
and still it is only   the bottom half of something.
No wonder my father   shed his   too-short pants
and went east.   Wasn't he craving the horizontal?
Gun to those who know it; gone to those who don't.

Kansas

Flatter than a chessboard. Held in place
by four winds struggling against each other. Vast as
the dining room table stretching in all directions
between us. Missouri's creamer and hovering
grandma of America urging, "Eat, Eat." Keeper
of cars that broke down on their way to the coasts.
Puzzle of my childhood, with one piece missing.

A Lesson in Fractions

My father cuts the last square of casserole in half and eats.
He cuts the half in half and eats again,

repeating this compulsive act like a school teacher
demonstrating an immutable mathematical truth.

Master of division, of less-than, he moves in measured bites
in the infinite direction of small,

while my mother wishes the meal would go on and on,
table expanding leaf after leaf into the cosmos,

large enough for children and grandchildren, dead parents and grandparents,
her sweet, overflowing kugel of a heart.

Meanwhile, my father has now whittled the square to a crumb
which he flattens with his knife into two halves,

one of which he lifts on his finger and eats.
"There are starving children in Europe," his mother said

and my father, ever obedient, can't let leftovers alone,
to this day can't stop until he's licked the table clean.

Still, he never takes the last piece, small rebellion against an equation
stunning in its inevitable conclusion:

A starving child in Europe will have one less brussels sprout
because a 10-year-old boy in Oregon did not eat his.

And so he halves and halves, dutifully eating,
seditiously bequeathing a crumb of solidarity

to all other children of children of immigrants,
meticulously, unconsciously, sacrificing the remains to the god of waste.

My father, wearing the same jeans he wore in high school,
still that thin and that frugal, sits quietly at the dinner table

and in sly, precisely executed strokes of the butterknife
commits his one selfish act.

Shooting the Square

Lawrence, Kansas

We drove round the night streets
in your parents' Ford Grenada

waiting to be seen.
We pretended it was otherwise.

It's hard to even wish for
what you know you don't deserve.

The world was too big for us,
we nailed it down to 4 corners.

We wanted to be seen as other people,
not how we saw ourselves.

The streets were ours to name:
23rd, Massachusetts, 6th and Iowa.

Tonight we would give our hearts
wholly to anyone.

That's what John Cougar was
telling us and we needed to believe.

We'd do the cheap cologne version
of love. It was all we could afford.

Say we were the brothers Grimm
collecting stories from the dark

to tell ourselves later,
about how we were wanted.

3 boys from Oskaloosa.
The blue Blazer. Your first kiss.

Then all the long nights
of nothing but each other

reading the backs of Harlequins
at Safeway at midnight.

Say we were 2 lonely Edens
formed side by side,

2 creation myths turned toward
opposite windows in search

of another. The cassette player
thumping between our thighs.

Calling it a night was just like
a little suicide.

You had never been kissed by anyone
not even your mother.

I had never been kissed by anyone
who meant it.

Was it a Bronco or a Blazer?
If only we could give our hearts wholly.

Just for the act of giving
and being received.

Tashlich

And you will cast all their sins into the depths of the sea.
—Micah 7:20

Let me toss these
sin sandwiches
in the water,
wrongs ribboned
through the bread.
Let them be
the opposite
of fortune cookies:

>   *May this never happen*
>   *May this never happen*
>   *May this never happen*

Water, I want
to return.
Wash clean
this residue of regret—
how I tried to be
visible through
the wounds graffitied
on my body:

>   *Jxxxxxa was here*
>   *Jxxxxxa was here*
>   *Jxxxxxa was here*

Erase it all
to be again
as on the day
I was born
skin transparent
as fingernail
my true name
shining through

Untitled 1954/55

Not the shock of unrestrained cacophonous
color exposed like the innards of an animal
still breathing, or the white walls cast in less
white lights, the whispered voices and a single bench.

Rather, how a home nested in their emptiness,
riotous spillover adrift in cirrostratus space,
so exposed it was as if I had a right to be
there. No need to explain the pied eruption:

collaged letters and papers, soft pink scribbles,
surplus blocks of stacked wood on saturated orange
and blue prints, the yellow and black seepage
that are my daily risings-up and lyings-down.

For a moment I could lean myself
against the side of the walled room
and frame my life, precisely as it is,
untitled, sloppily textured, still wet.

I let go the desire to feel desire, or just to feel,
that sets teens red-lining the secret diaries
of their thighs and stomachs with precise cuts,
twisting the knob right off Too Much.

A chilled bowl of summer pea soup
at the café across from Yerba Buena Gardens
drizzles from the spoon as if in bright green
conversation with Rauschenberg's Untitled 1954/55.

I am not entwined on the grassy square with my lover
or riding a bike through the streets of San Francisco,
a messenger bag slung over my shoulder with a place to go.
It isn't that kind of painting. It isn't that kind of day.

After the laying on of hues, the stripping back,
the exquisite less that is somehow more, like the city
mirrored in a puddle slicked with oil, I visit the Calders,
remember two steel goats I'd pass under

on my way to the *shuk* in Jerusalem, yellow and angular
against a blue sky and graphite green olive branches.
I'd pass them again on the way back, bags full
of small, round eggplants, persimmons, lemons,

paprika, and a loaf of freshly baked bread,
one bag in each hand to balance
as I trudged the high grass beside the train tracks
until they ran too far ahead and out of sight.

On Becoming a Woman

for my daughter on her 12th birthday

The sunflowers die, their yellow suns plucked
to blank masks, the petals wilted collars.

The figs grow, hard-bellied green bells now.
Daily walks, we measure ourselves

against these gardens, you seeking out
almost-ripe blackberries, small lemons.

Seasons leave their marks: Leaves turn red,
figs stain the sidewalk, there are irises

or not, sour grass or not, but nothing is ever
not changing, not renewing. Like my body,

my own yard is so untended its changes
are no longer noticeable, dry, cracked earth

and shriveled bushes, overgrown roses,
arthritic limbs twisted to pillars of salt.

Periods come reluctantly, rarely, like guests
in a pandemic. The blood, if at all, is dark

and clotted or falsely bright and thin, too much
or too little, a meal prepared by an angry cook.

They say it's a sort of death, and it feels that way,
as if the body is emptying, caving in on itself,

breast drooping, belly extending down
where a baby once rounded and filled.

Sexuality dries up, closing shop on fertility,
that goddess potential, sistering moon and tides.

But who told us to be woman
means to be a bearer of children?

Who decides what is an end and what is a beginning?
Birth, puberty, marriage, any moment of change turns

on the direction we look. Lot's wife turned to stone
by looking back. Face it. The body lies.

All the stories it told me growing up, of my unworth.
The lies your body tells you, refuting the girl

you have always been. You ask
when you can start hormones to grow breasts.

I buy a dozen bras, two dozen teardrop pads.
You caress them like small pets, put them back

in the drawer. You are a girl who won't bleed.
To become a woman, you give up fertility.

Forty-four years apart we shed skins, shed stories,
we give birth to ourselves. Look at the lemon tree.

See how everything grows in its own time,
at the same time, white blossoms, knotted green nubs,

yellow fruit large enough to fill your growing hands.
My daughter, my beautiful blossom, do you see?

As you grow into the woman you are,
I am becoming the mother you need.

The Apple Tree and the Fig Tree

The apples shiver at the top of the tree.
It hurts me how small they are,
fisted red balls,
how sure of themselves.

Beside them the figs crawl over one another
like newborn pups and the fat leaves
hang loosely, as if sin
had not yet been invented.

So much is growing:
figs, apples, cells, spirit, light,
the changes rapid and undetectable
in the white morning breeze.

Except there, up in the hills,
the way the fog is beginning to curl
as if the sky were a canvas
we could roll back with our hands.

Alight

To question is to break with something;
it is to establish an inside and an outside.

—Edmond Jabès, *Du Desert au Livre*

Hamsah

I was so small. How could I ask?
There were no words for what was not
already full-grown inside me.

A simple gesture: Turn the wrist. Uncurl the fingers.
The night so vast against my open palm,
the heart exposed—how can I hold it?

The night sustains itself.
I learn that what is whole weighs nothing.
Desire reaches beyond its hunched boundaries

and the wanting opens still more,
stepping over the old measurements chalked
in the locked house of childhood.

I stake down the roots of this new site. I claim
the birthright of the third daughter, stolen
by her sisters, her child-mother, her own invisibility.

For the first time she outgrows the little pink room,
its one wall of flowers, its one wall of fear
the strip of light pulsing under the door.

Now I want everything: the moonlight
spilling onto the neighbor's porch,
that laughter, the air's cool touch.

In this black pool of yard, the porch is a ship.
The stairway down to the fig tree, to the black,
blossoming apple tree does not touch ground.

I hold this thin, gold hand in mine,
its heart-pressed palm turned up.
If I can slow my breath to its cadence,

acclimate my body to darkness,
I will undress from all my desires
into infinite, weightless arms.

Safety Matches

Silver cylinder.
Made in Hong Kong.

For soldiers or scouts.
Six matches sealed inside.

I keep my spirit for safekeeping,
drawn to the small, the locked, the secret.

I wish I could be held in one hand.

What if these matches were lit?
Sacrificed to a candle or cigarette,

a quick speck of light on the dark?
What is so sacred about safety?

A legacy of events that did not happen,
were not ignited:

The six times you were not
lost, the six times you did not

find yourself alone in need of light.
Passed down:

Here, take these.
Do not burn.

Hidden, my soul waits to be struck.

One for love,
to catch suddenly.

One for clarity,
to see myself and my way.

One for change,
a toast to what is yet unseen.

One for destiny,
follow wood to flame and leap.

One for faith in the after-light.
One to leave no trace.

What, then, is seven?
The empty vessel

resting place
for a tiny scroll of good,

the hair of a loved one,
a cache of sand and stones.

If I burn them, who will open me?

Remember the head of the match,
red against crisscrosses of silver:

hiss, snap, flame,
blue heart of twisting ghost-fire,

the burning, the dying out,
spark, ember, memory,

the birth of a different kind of darkness:
the kind in which there once was light.

Yehi Or (And There Was Light)

> And God made the two great lights: the greater light to rule the
> day, and the lesser light to rule the night, and the stars.
> —Genesis 1:15

At 3 a.m. I went in search of the lesser light that rules the night according to the Bible,
and the second brightest light in the night sky according to *USA Today*.

I put on T-shirt, glasses, and shoes and believed myself the Invisible Man,
nothing more than the things themselves with night unimpeded between.

But when I stealthed from the house a flurry of lights popped up:
first the lamp left on in my bedroom window,

revealing a strange, superfluous scene
in which no one was sleeping in the bed.

Then one after another like a movie jailbreak, bang, bang, bang.
The porch, the yard, the stairs—lit, lit, lit.

Lights chased me down the black road and, as in a fairytale,
tricked me past the gates of safety.

There in the dark pool of road,
I felt the covert strength and height of my naked legs.

The brilliant half-moon punched a light in the sky not lesser than but equal to the sun—
the Bible got it wrong—just turned in on itself.

And in a web of sticky, numberless stars, Mars—*USA Today* got it right—
was one bright orange piercing, closer than it's been for 50,000 years.

So there we were.
Forming some new constellation:

Half-moon   Mars

    the empty bedroom

                a woman   6 lit steps.

None of us were close enough.

Did other constellations feel this?
Allied but estranged?

The handle of Ursa Major
longing to taste the milky soup in the bowl,

Orion's hand itching
for the distant grip of his sword?

I wanted to taste the moon's pale, graveled curves,
to flesh Mars out from dry red riverbeds of dust.

Instead I followed the 6 lit steps like luminous crumbs
across the lit yard, into the house, back

to the bright, abandoned room.
There I showed the moon and Mars my lesser light.

Inside the Room, Outside the Night

A kettle whistles on the other side of the wall,
3 barks from a dog thump the black night,
but inside it's just 3 bulbs and a slow-ticking clock
ventriloquist heart throwing its voice to the windowsill.

Like the moon held up to the ear,
I listen quietly for myself
she's in here somewhere—under books,
between voices and lost scents through the windows.

Let each wall tell the story of safety as if it were new,
grow 4 mothers in the telling:
safe says the 2-windowed wall against the garden,
safe the double-lamped wall concurs, like 2 eyes watching over my bed.

Safe, safe, safe say the 3 windows on the next wall.
Even the wall's story made of closet doors ends happily.
Inside myself it's night-quiet, night-dark,
as if these were the real windows of the room:

2 eyes, nose, mouth, and, below, vagina
with its wrinkled, folded drapes—5 windows
leading to the dark, infinite outsideness of in.
Is this why I never fit, walking around inside out,

trying to gain entrance, when all the doors open inward?
Imagine dissipating, refracting through the windows,
5 selves knocking at the glass asking their way
back to the lamp and the wide-hipped bed with its flowered pillows.

Who wouldn't return to such softness and weight?
But another runaway self rises up and is gone,
thinning to the language of air, tagging the mountains and sky,
ecstatic to be free of body, never going back to that tired jail-shell.

Come back. Come back to the little room
with its equidistant corners, its matriarchal walls.
We'll do the square dance of identity,
dosie-doe rabbi and doubter, poet and daughter,

swing your superego round and around,
promenade the bad girl who slid grown-up books
down the side of the bed. Stop. Quiet the clock.
Let the heart choose her own pace and swell:

brushstrokes smoothing the scalp, cherries
dropped one by one into a tea-toweled bowl,
that kind of Albuquerque rain that evaporates
before it ever touches ground.

A Question of Night

When the night
          loves me
               offering its stars
                  like grapes
                     as I lie
                       dizzying
                          below them
                            changing
                              and exchanging
                            hierarchies
                          I lay down
                            my questions.
                          The night
                          cools
                            so still
                            it might
                              not exist
                                couldn't
                              exist
                                with so little
                              weight in it
                            flat shadows
                        of trees
                     moths
                  writing
                longhand
             on air
            almost nothing
          so thinly winged
        so little of them
       that is not wing.
      Other times
     I sense
    the night's
   indifference
  how deep
 the gap
how beneath
I am. I ask
to be let in
the asking
lies arced

between us
the night outside
the poem outside
myself this kernel
of hardness
fisting me from
the order of things
small pushings
on tender bruises
white holes
between words
the only hope
to reconcile
particulars.
Could I be
star-like
or a stone lost
in the dark or
what is lifting
the leaves
off the necks
of trees
disperse into
particles
of light the
spaces in-
between?
Infinity inches
in the direction
of in.
A question
ladders
itself down
the way we
bow God
into being
inner and
outer dipped
in the same
black bath
body awash
neither forgotten
nor remembered
the way I
neither forget

nor remember
my scars
or the thin bones
of my arms
the mind
bigger than this
tiny me-part
bigger than stone
or stars
the mind cogged
in eternal
mechanisms
it can't begin
to understand:

    Doesn't
  the universe
 question, also?
How else can it
    expand?

My Father's Study

on the 20th anniversary of 9/11 and my father's 9th yartzeit

Speak directly to the moon. Not family. Not God.
Only the moon defines herself irrespective of events.

Lie back in the black crescent, his easy chair.
Where my father escaped, listening to Coltrane.

Bookshelves still tall and articulate, fairytale towers
of Freud, Matisse, Galápagos, Judaism, Jazz.

Of daughters: clay figures in a rowboat, three
under falls at Yosemite, three biting a baguette in Gay Paree.

Outside the window, the moon gets tangled in pear trees.
THE LITTLE PRINCE in Hebrew, TALES OF RABB NACHMAN OF BRESLOV.

Gaps in the dark.
Places where place ought to be.

Read out loud. Relentless in the silence.
Sound out words like *tel-e-skop* טלסקופ.

The snake swallows—*bole'a* בולע from *liv'loa* לבלוע—the *pil* פיל
elephant, first words learned in the basement of the JCC.

Swallow whole paragraphs without comprehension.
Hebrew and English not noticing each other in the brain.

Just words. Just letters.
Just one lighted room on a dark street.

A story: The little shepherd who wants to pray so he recites the alphabet.
His prayers ascend to heaven; he sits on the Rabbi's lap.

The moon higher now.
Branches touching with nothing in their grasp.

Consonants like towers that can topple.
Vowels underneath like commentary, or the dead.

California Oak Moths

Last night she rose to pee
fumbling in the dark for the light
and there in the clawfoot tub
a world revealed itself to her.

Moths alight on the white curtains,
moths opening and closing their slight wings
on the dry bed of this drained pond,
one or two still fluttering, circling above.

They were the moths of dreams,
their pale, abalone wings pearled
and textured in the complex patterns
of vintage lace. They must have confused

the stark white cleanness of porcelain
with light, the way we sometimes confuse purity
with good. She wanted to draw their attention
from the virginal gleam of the bath

its metaphysical perfection of emptiness
to her own shimmering and hard-earned light,
subtle but seeping into aura, she hoped,
into something like a halo.

Confuse me with the moon, she said,
believe yourselves to have reached that bright Mecca,
the crescent fold of my white body
on the toilet, my soul's lamp lit.

Alight, alight, and I will confuse you in return
with God, luck, lovers, manna, a muse:
anything I ever wanted to seek me out
that burned in me instead.

Arterials

The night rings moons around my wrist
a planetary system protecting the blood
full moon white of the pale inner arm
where veins trace milky and blue,
a galaxy just visible under the skin.

The blood longs to escape.
Enough of this mapped course of what it is
to be alive, enough of marked journeys.
The cells yearn to redirect, orbit other worlds,
dodge the predictable circulation of limbs.

When we divorce from the world it goes on without us,
constellations intact, planets braceleting the sun.
It takes the stars and their shapes with it,
takes the magnitude of night and joy in little things.
It leaves the little things.

Havdalah

Was it evening or night
when our hearts sank down below the horizon
and neither of us trusted

they would rise again?
The grass went dark
on one side of the hill

and because I could not stop
the shadow spreading
I thought I was its source.

We didn't talk about it.
It's boring to tell your dreams
and we were stuck in them.

Like Adam on his first nightfall
crying *Surely darkness comes to bruise me!*
we thought it would be night forever.

With no one to teach us
to spark two flints into one flame
we had only the separation.

Nothing changed outside of ourselves.
It's the same grass, like you said.
No amount of stars would matter.

So we drank cheap Carmel wine,
ate a last meal of stale bread and bruised figs
high up on the ruins of the Citadel

and watched the Kineret go dark.
Long before the 982 bus snaked its way
down to Jerusalem, we had taken our leave.

Entrance to the Letter *Aleph*

א

Root of my faith and root of my rebellion
tugging the underearth of my heart.

My voice keeps running away
into faithless, foreign words

that all begin with I
as if you

were not breathing
even this vowel into me.

You are a door that joins,
and through joining, divides

my knock not even
an echo of you.

I beat myself against your white silence
hear it rattle whisper-thin like rice paper.

How I've come to love your blank, muscled skin
the way it mutes and softens my anger.

Don't answer.
Don't answer.

It's enough to lean and rest awhile.
Enough to trace these black-hewn houses

their tiny hidden lights
and eternal yearnings

enough to turn their corners
and seek.

Cardamom and Myrrh

Sugar scatters the white cloth in service.
I place myself by the door, in the way of calling.

Here are two more roses in the world not given to me.
Here an empty chair for a hungry god.

The one I love loves Jesus.
He serves spiced chicken and milky tea.

Sometimes we must take off our shoes,
trust the holy ground black-beading under our feet.

Why does my faith split in two before this darkened glass?
Why do I love the world more when it goes on without me?

Jesus was stretched and angular, I am full,
fleshed like the baby or the nursing mother,

too much for such civility.
He brings a tin bowl to wash my hands, a subtle baptism.

I stir the sugar in my tea with the daintiest spoon.
My wrists at least are suitable, beat like throats of birds.

Inside the *Genizah*

Three walls that asked no questions
one window that let in wind and voice but not winter

Deserts that opened until my walls folded flat
then stretched into blue wings and took flight

Nameless angels who left me unnamed
a tiger orchid—*oncidium splendidum*—the color of flesh

A stranger's hand in a plush theater
the sudden thirst to hold and protect another's skin

The falling place at 3 a.m. that is God
and the not being caught that is God

Alphabets writing themselves on the whites of books
burning alphabets, smudged letters forbidden to discard

Letters locked in attics for torn centuries
broken words stashed too long in the body's ark

Two Dreams at Beth-El

It's a black night with wind
and the leaves shrinking back on the trees.
Something pushes up through my body
like a slow, rising sap. This alive,
my body falls away like dying petals,
just like that.

Let's name it what it is: an evil birth,
an old shame, probably not mine.
The stars drift outside the window
like blessings that will never come to be.
This is the dream: no ladders
to ascend or descend, no angels
arranging themselves like Chinese letters
inking slowly down the sky.
Just a soul set free like a lost balloon.
Just a nameless stone knocking
at the base of my neck.

My soul ascends the ladder
but I don't ascend.
I stay with the sleeping body
tethered to a rock,
watch the angels go up and down
like someone at an airport
with time to kill.
Even after the sun
the soul does not come back.
I dream of its absence,
a hollow, crumbling dream
that won't wake itself.

Rio Caliente

Darkness untongues the day
condensed to obsidian in its silent belly.
Turn away from the world and be the night.
Let it slip in you as if dipped in liquid soul, the body nothing
you should concern yourself with now, the body a house
you stepped out of into this forest of your beginning.

Let the currents guide you.
Let the river teach you your sinews and bones.
Ask the dense spaces between trees to open to you.
Ask the breeze to muss the veil of dark.
Ask the blanketed sky to open one eye to the moon.
Ask what sings in you that rocks the stars to sleep.

Who will answer if you wrestle the night
as if it were your brother wounding you to a new self
beside a twisting river its black body snake-like and hot?
Ask the night to bless you   ask the night your name
ask the night to call itself and surrender to its telling
syllables falling wet off the mountains.

The world spins slowly so that even words settle and sink.
Only the river speaks swift and black
fluting a cord of sound through the thick fields of morning
polishing silence off the palms of stones
bearing your name on its currents
through the dark alphabets of sleep.

Notturno in D

Arad, Israel

Every night it is the same.
The square is deserted.
I wish for a heavier coat.
The clouds drift apart.

*

Slowly night wrings all the color out of things.
A cluster of *haredim* like blackbirds rush by.
Their long coats flap in the wind.

An American woman walks her poodle.
I have made three phone calls at the public payphones, pretending.
I know you are there.

The last teenage boys leave the theater.
Everything is just as far as it appears.
I have no reason to be here.

*

The desert is erasing itself on all sides.
Sometimes a dried leaf, sometimes a Coke bottle
        rolls, rolls, rolls, stops.

*

Almost midnight: you begin to stack the chairs.
When your eye catches mine it happens suddenly:
Bedouin bracelets clenching in on the wrist.

It is not what you think.
It is the moon.
It is the emptiness.

I forget which mask I am wearing,
walk home in someone else's body.
Sleep in someone else's dreams.

*

When we meet, it is Purim.
My costume is the moon.

You drink two Goldstars, pretending.
We speak your language, then mine.

I steal a picture of you from your wallet while you sleep.
Already the wanting has lessened.

The night must be finished
like a bitter medicine that will not cure.

Just to be sure, I never once call you
by your given name.

Miriam's Skin

And the cloud turned from the Tent and there was
Miriam, stricken with leprosy like snow.
—Numbers 12:10

One drapes over the other
dark smoke streaming pale skin
light presses seeking entry
until I begin to sense myself
as home to One who loves me
drenched light one yearns to get inside
and if a cloud must burn itself across
in search of that well
who am I to say no
who am I to say anything
when words come to rest
like the braided prints of birds
or the last winter twigs on snow
who am I to say   who am I
limbs stretched in four directions
a voice transcribing my spine
lacing my hips, making maps

Sonnet for Habib Koité

Strum a sticky summer night
net a lover in the webs of your arms
hips, hips, we were given feet

hips, hips, we were given feet
to hold our hips up, necks to narrow
fanning to flesh-wings where ball and femur meet

it's funny how music makes us forget
where our ears are
hips hips we were given feet

hips hips we were given feet
opens new buttons under our skin,
flutters the heart sync beat on beat

hips, hips: who will make love as good as this guitar?
hips, hips: who will feed chilled mangos in the dark?

Questions for My Tibetan Healer

Is there a drumbeat louder than this whirlwind loss?
Am I in a Hitchcock movie? Am I? Am I? The birds
are feeding at my ear. Will magic work when
I stop poking around for who is fooling me?
Who taught me to hate myself this way?
Did I? Did I? Why didn't I fill in the holes
of their love with love of my own?
Can you cleanse me with 5 notes in the throat?
Can you? Can you? When I love myself,
the dark parts shake out into the universe.
The rivers run black. Is there a note
for every finch? A finch for every word?
When I know that God is, will I have always known?

Bath and Afterbath

The Bath

Walls slipping down into water
      like silk
            sliding to the floor
the whole world
      not just its pieces
            bathed in candlelight
all presences
      moving toward
            a center I only suspected

What isn't white
      shoots prisms
            through the water
my body
      revealed as beautiful
            the woman rising up to meet her skin
as if I could be desirable
      as if desiring myself
            were enough
when I always believed
      there had to be two
            to be one

But look
      I've pulled the other
            out of myself
my rib not his
      and with it I stroke
            and recreate myself
new sides sprouting
      trailing like wings
            out of the bath

The Afterbath

Rested
  after so long a journey
    in search of one country
where I can sink myself
  into water
    lose my body in flame
where the stars
  still carve out
    the same formations
and the shadow
  of my writing hand
    traces the wall

Something enters
  as I trusted it would
    the rain etching my name
on the windows
  like the crinkling
    of an old phonograph
Reminiscence, I say
  loving the word
    though I have nothing
to remember
  the water
    forgetting everything

As if I were beautiful
  as if I did not know
    where my body ended
the softest drowning
  of a self
    into herself
the beast unspelled
  words coming loose
    then unraveling

Summoning the *Shechinah*

Hands dipped white,
words and measurements laid out
on the counter before me

> I will you into our world.
> Impossibly weighted,
> three-dimensional

I will your shimmering particles into water,
knead you condensed and pliant,
amazed at your own resilience.

> You are warm,
> caressed and battered
> by so many asking hands

you grow soft,
allow yourself
to be lovingly braided.

> Now you stretch and rise
> into the thick wonder of physical form;
> you harden a skin of your own.

This Sabbath may you dwell with us,
in us, under a white cloth roof,
rooted, still reaching.

> You are the sweetness in our mouths,
> the hope that one day
> we can reverse the incantation:

take the heaviness of who we are
and knead it back
into light.

Nobody's Apple

Wherever the apple tree goes, its offspring propose so many different variations on what it means to be an apple—at least five per apple, several thousand per tree—that a couple of these novelties are almost bound to have whatever qualities it takes to prosper in the tree's adopted home.

—Michael Pollan, *The Botany of Desire: A Plant's-Eye View of the World*

Late Afternoon at Café Roma

Day tilts down toward evening,
last of the sun glancing
off glass, everything at an angle,

like a turned-down bed.
Inside, I offer myself like an apple.
New scarf, new book, new dress, new shoes.

Tell me, young men,
haven't you ever
seen ripeness?

Lights tossed up to the ceiling
shine from where they struck,
the room a little Mozart universe.

I should leave before the windows
double my solitude—
Who said I was forbidden?—

before I can no longer see
the last Christmas lights
wrap white snakes around trees.

Today I am nobody's apple.
Like the late sun
or a new moon

too early rising, I
am the one who desires—
subject, not object—

full night
for which the day
must fall.

Twilight's Poem, Dawn-Written

> To what may twilight be compared? Rabbi Tanhuma said:
> To a drop of blood placed on the tip of a sword: the instant
> it takes the drop to divide into two parts, that is twilight.
> —Talmud

5 a.m.

The trees take back their shapes.
I am vigilant.
All night the shadow of a mountain
marked the mountain's place
and now the mountain is back, heavy,
stubbled with trees that in an hour will be green
a millennia of rock that will dazzle red.
It looks like creation, I know, but it isn't.
Dawn is the moment of fissure
when we take our leave of beginnings
settle deeper into our bodies
rigid if that's what we are
animated if that's what we are
hurting if that's what we are.

Last night I tried to go back
to pinpoint the exact moment
the world began, built on the premise
of precipice: *It was evening it was morning*
וַיְהִי־עֶרֶב וַיְהִי־בֹקֶר
neither this nor that
and I, longing always for beginnings
want to slip sideways
into that slit between day and night
back to the whole
before the blood split on the sword
before there had to be two
of everything.

7 p.m.

Already lights pierce neat holes in houses.
Rocks leap up white as bones
geraniums spilling red drops all over
the dying light
coolness a salve on the day's mistakes
as the daisies are reborn
radiant, baptismal

each center the center of the universe,
golden eye of the garden.
And you can hear things beginning, too,
at the end of the day, sounds rubbing
against the silent places
creak and dog bark
my footsteps precise and solid
like the first footsteps all others must have copied
Ayekah? אַיֶּכָּה The Voice in the garden: Where are you?
wanting to be asked.

What I am seeking is something like indistinction
when day and night are inseparable
creator and created merged
and my capacity to distinguish
this from that, to make separations
binah בינה, understanding, from *bein* בֵּין, between,
pools into *tohu va'vohu* תֹּהוּ וָבֹּהוּ swimming in the deep.

6 a.m.

Papers scatter like wings across the white bed,
books turn their names away from me
their delicate inner pages bared.
Today I will rise and eat the reddest fruit
just to be bad

just to be one thing over another.
It is too much, trying to remember
how to be whole.

This is why I watch for dawn,
the moment of complete separation
my life falling from the tree
into my own hands.

7 a.m. at the Western Wall

7 a.m. at the Wall the men
eddy and swirl, wearing their prayers
on their sleeves. Angry old men with long beards
shout against the wall
as if it were a donkey
blocking the road.

7 a.m. at the Wall the women
rock and sway in heavy black shoes
moving their lips to silent music.
Tired old women kiss the wall
as if it were a long-lost child
setting out again.

Answer us! demand the men
pounding the door to their King.

Speak to us, implore the women
whispering to their Lover
across a pillow of stone.

All These Gaps

You can slow the day down, but you can't stop it.

I've tried, sitting in the Red Café with fingers of jazz
running up and down my brass ribcage.
Thinking of all the ways to be touched that I am not.

I am searching for some kind of consistency.
Proof that if I hold out my hand someone
will put something in it, even a hand of their own.

I am writing my way through the day to hold it back,
through the close-tipped flowers and the green stem
widening in the beaded glass as the bright morning

pushes through the stucco of buildings across the street.
I can write dense like this but who will want it?
Who will want me now with all these gaps?

And who dressed me this way when I feel so otherwise?
Who arranged us in this order at our little round tables?
With all the windows and mirrors.

What am I humming to the world that keeps it away?
Is this the usual hurt or is it unique,
the only hurt of its kind?

Meanwhile, I keep willing myself upright,
long enough to remember why we do it this way,
why forward is the required direction.

Mud Soup

Bay Area Discovery Museum, Sausalito

Mask over mouth mutes her pen.
What needs to be named on a day
so California calm it is barely of this world?

Cars on the bridge glide silently by, as do
wisped clouds, steelhead trout in the bay,
bubbles pushed through a sieve by the breeze.

Like drops of blood under a microscope, children
spray-paint crimson watercolors
on a sheet tacked to the wall, spilled Kool-Aid.

What needs to be named? That xylophone wind
awakening the pines? The fog-veiled Golden Gate?
Wind, wake me, too. Unmask us both.

Lay my sinews and veins across a fluttering sheet
and call it art. Call it woman. Call it Yiskah.
Leave the body over there, on a bench, asleep.

Then who will call the wire cables
looming the bridge Strings on a Harp?
Who will call this child stirring mud soup

with tin ladles Hope? Or just Dirt-under-Nails Alive?
Who will ask if the bubbles rising past the red roofs
interrupt the sky or become one with it?

What would this day be without her gaze,
the geometric trestles crisscrossed under the bridge
just industrial steel without metaphor, the hills

at peace, soothed by the voices of children,
little hands clutching spoons and plastic crabs,
raking mallets over the backs of frogs?

If her questions float past the pines and disappear
will this, whether she names it or not, letting
the day nap cradled in salt and fog, be happy?

Perfect Paring

Apple. Not too
large. Palm.
Not too small.

Arch carved
crisp white
with teeth.

Ragged moon
knocked off
the red planet.

Concaved,
a C
to lie down in.

Barefoot daughter
invisible in
daylight.

Whole fruit
forgotten
by motherhood.

A mother's craft:
Pare. Puree.
Quarter and dice.

Slice sideways
with seeded stars
on special days.

After,
alone.
Half-

moon
above trees,
blanket pinned

by shoes,
two large,
two small.

Permission
as woman
to devour whole,

savagely snap
after so many
neat knives.

Why bring
just one?
Feed me

another.
I want five.
Backpack brimming,

even the shoes
crammed suddenly
with apples.

Mother tongue
made up
pairings:

Good, bad.
Empty, full.
Honey, crisp.

Language
like all living things
evolves,

outgrows
its origins,
that first

palmed planet
now blushed
by distance.

But a mouth
never forgets
such taste,

as the apple
never forgets
the tree.

New Moon of the Month of *Nissan*

In the sea that is the garden
walling the east side of my house,
miracles happen in spring.

Witness from my bedroom window:
Irises that were not blue-feathered birds
brushing the fence, are now.

Even when my feet beg, I don't go down.
Inner enemies weed up their chariots,
closing me in.

Daily the garden splits me open.
Moses says, *Be still.*
Branches glitter and green with voice.

All night the rain shakes her tambourines.
Morning my anxious dreams drown
in the sudden light.

At the garden's gate I leave my shoes,
carry only thin moons,
unrisen futures asleep on my back.

Meridian

Newly scaped, the needles mark
places on my back for breaking ground.
I am leaving; my house must travel.
She draws shapes all over my body
until I am something like sky.

Porcupined, fairy-wounded, I hunch to the mirror
to see those sleek silver arrows
angled into skin like hard summer rain.
Such soft round flesh, such thin, hard points,
a treacherous terrain conquered and flagged.

The needles speak to each other, their voices buzzing
like light passed back and forth, across and down.
I am the ball tossed between their long fingers,
the shadow of the ball crisscrossing the grass,
the warm, damp grass canvassing light and shadow.

I dream-walk the cartographer's journey
find messages left between mountains, under stones.
I am a tree awakened by small birds,
a lover roused by light kisses—shoulder blade,
inside of wrist, back of knee, arch of foot.

The needles slip out easy as dawn.
Button shirt, buckle watch, put on one shoe and the next,
disguised in the stuff of the tangible world,
the sleeping world to which I have, at last, awakened
or which I will, at last, awaken, point by point, kiss by kiss.

A Woman Asks to Be Named

Speak me.
Let my name be gossiped by stars
travel light-years to its next exchange
all that silence still trailing.

Speak me.
Let my body be knitted by roots
scripting my limbs with skeins
of feathered dark.

Speak me the way you spoke
light into being, the way you moved
dark aside
as if it were nothing.

Speak me the way you spoke
the very first of us from dust
mouth to mouth.
I know you remember.

Speak me as if I were
that new, that needed
garden tiller, rainmaker, helpmeet,
sabbath to rest inside.

Speak me.
I have represented myself poorly.
I am not a mouth filled with dirt.
I am not a final letter sealed in its end.

Etch me the way you carved
Anochi אנוכי on tablets of stone
white fire on black fire
your mouth to his hand.

Brush the first fine point of me
here or there
ink-seed in the infinite palm:
I am.

Desert Is a Mouth Opening

Desert is a mouth opening

the beginning of all words
I only speak to finish

bouncing questions back
into the cups of my hands

and I drink.

*

Desert is a mouth opening

an unlicked stamp
anticipating attachment

sending souls flying
to the other side of the zipcode

in their slender white suits.

*

Desert is a mouth opening

unable to bite down
on a single consonant

a forever expanse
into the possibility of language

any words, any words
you choose to pray.

Techelet

In the fringes of the *tallit* a blue thread once fell,
crushed from the shell of a desert snail.
Nobody knows its true color anymore.
In this packed synagogue, in this century,
I try to conjure *techelet*, that mythic hue
to make room as room was made
for women to pray with men, for a blue
that is not the blue of any blue thing we know.
Why I can't thread a single strand of mystery
through the eye of my constricted mind?
Instead I tug the white yarns one by one
counting, naming, knotting, worrying
them like rosaries, frayed jeans.

It's different when *davenning* alone
under the knotted branches of an aging oak,
hips bowing and swaying.
My *tzitzit* fall loose in the wind, flutter
like ribbons in my daughter's hair, water
twisting down the sides of mountains,
the first unveiled glances of desire.
Dangling reinventions of grasping fingers
that always aim to keep what they find,
my *tzitzit* are flippers diving me deep.
They are the blue-gray wings of doves
flying to the four corners of the Earth
to bring home peace in slender brown beaks.

Learning the Essentials

עֶצֶם (*etzem*): bone; thing, object; essence, the very
—*Oxford Hebrew-English Dictionary*

My father's body is teaching him how to die.
That's what bodies do. They instruct.

It wants to lie down. It is practicing.
Thinner and thinner, it begins to let go

of muscle and memory
all but the essentials.

It is forgetting taste, forgetting how to walk.
Forgetting what it means to forget.

He knows us. He loves us. But his body teaches him
how not to want, how not to need.

When he was a teacher, my father investigated
how language begins, how babies learn to talk,

the precise moment they recognize their mother's voice.
Now he is learning how language ends,

how it unravels its way back
to an ocean of groans and harsh breathing.

The body is the teacher now.
My father assumes the role of student.

But he is not always a good student.
Like today, when tears river his papery cheeks

and he won't let go the little grandchild in his arms.
Or when he puts on his thirty-year-old Birkenstocks

and shuffles the hall with a nurse and a walker
singing the same marching songs he taught us

hiking to Green Lake summers in Oregon,
the ones he learned as a Boy Scout.

Other days, he is a star pupil.
We talk as if he isn't there, he is so still.

And what about the living?
What do our bodies teach us?

We bustle around,
restless bedpan messes of need and want.

Fear rattles our bones so loud
my father can't sleep for the grinding noise of it.

We commandeer the cafeteria,
hold long discussions

about what's for lunch, nurse
the disappointment of little plums that taste like stones.

My child sits on the floor sorting puzzles
from the hospital gift shop, farm animals and trains.

Sometimes she stomps around in my father's shoes,
making everyone laugh.

My father completes his schooling,
lays down in the earth to rest.

In the small Jewish cemetery
surrounded by cornfields and church crosses,

I listen to how each cascade of dirt over the casket
forms a soft jazz rhythm like the scratch of brushes on drums.

I recite the prayers of mourning. Add my own fist of dirt
to fulfill the mitzvah of burying the dead.

My child runs wild between the gravestones.
I don't stop her.

Her body is teaching her,
teaching us, how to live.

Birdwatcher

Inside a stone, river.
Inside a woman, grief.
Held, it flowers.
Flowering, it dies.

Dying, it bears fruit
until grief is all she knows
a lens to catch the world
and make it slow.

The birds won't be still.
They strut in full color
across the dark lens
flit in and out of its small frame,

crying, "Faith. Faith."
Round as tiny suns they circle
swallowing grief's fruit
in quick beaks.

Inside a stone, river.
Inside a woman, sky.
River and sky.
River and wings and sky.

The Morning After a Vipassana Retreat

Always sit by the south window
where the ferned stone staircase leads up,
eucalyptus trunks even more so, to see how
the magnolia blossoms contemplate attachment,
pink petals scattered on the dark ground.

Those twisted branches could be snakes,
succulents sewn from ribboned tongues.
Still, this garden tells no stories,
the vast left wall swathed
in hushed, green moss.

On the table, a bowl of thin porridge steams,
applesauce pooling its middle,
salt crunch of almonds, tart melt
of cubed cheddar, all this in one bowl,
one mouth, quietly chewing.

Conversations ring out
like the full-throated frogs in last night's pond,
a din not unlike silence in its thick uniformity.
If I were a small, egg-shaped stone in the garden,
no one would notice me but me.

Seventh Day in the Valley

Blue jays exchanged mating calls
hopping and swooping around me on the deck

raucous rattle and sweet *kuet kuet kuet*,
then flying branch to branch to start their nest.

Yellow roses made their final bows,
scattered patterned petals

in a path to the kitchen.
There I made a careful pot of tea.

The mountain was jagged in places,
soft in others, and magnificent.

As the sky darkened, the house
was as quiet as I'd ever known it.

Even the dictionary pressed its words
against flat red leaves in little kisses.

A coyote crossed the driveway,
then turned to watch.

We watched
each other.

We watched
a good, long while.

How I knew I had, at last,
grown still.

Alone on My Daughter's First Night of Sleepaway Camp

Jews do not bow down, not all the way to the ground.
I did. I don't mean on Yom Kippur, awkwardly crouched

among folding chair legs and purses, or under sequoias
with the Berkeley hippies on the new year for trees.

Or, okay, that one time at the Zen center in front of Buddha,
who isn't a god, and deserved it. I mean tonight, vanquished

by a sudden storm of gratitude, falling to my knees in a strange room
forehead pressed to the won't-show-the-dirt brown rug

between a child-size rocking chair stripped of its blue paint
and the unopened suitcase stuffed with my prior life.

And when that wasn't enough—when the fat,
female curves of my aging body could not fold flat

like the wings of my child's origami cranes to enact
from dust thou art and to dust thou shalt return—

I lowered myself all the way down, prostrate, smashed
in synthetic fibers, like when I lay at the roots of the redwood,

sank nose and cheeks in wet soil, and planted myself,
leaving a part of me still growing there, a woman whose life

forked a different angle, didn't lug home sperm
in a nitrous oxide tank and raise a child in middle age.

And when that wasn't enough, the curve of breasts
that once nursed my child to not needing to nurse squashed

against the floor like UPS air pillows preventing a full flush,
I flipped on my back like an otter, arms flung out in a cross,

sacrificial offering to the gods of gratitude, looking up
to bless each imperfect knot in the rough pine 2 x 4 ceiling

of this hand-built Tahoe vacation home, bless the heavy, raw,
unfinished cross beams, torn red velvet curtains on their broken rod,

almost lick the spindled leg of the rocking chair from love,
bless the small dead moths stacked at the bottom of the wall sconce

like a pile of neatly raked leaves, buried close to the light the way
we humans scatter ashes over a beloved garden or sea.

Sometimes the beauty of this world hits all at once like a hard slap.
The terrible things I have done, how I ooze out like broken yolk.

Then this foreign silence. This precise moment of grace.
How to wring out the layers of silt and sin,

the still-winged carcasses of error after error
to find a place for who I used to be but never was?

How to breadcrumb myself back to what I knew
when the doctor pulled my baby out from between bent knees

in one weirdly grand swoop like a magician and scarves,
that fierce and instant dissipation into joy and terror,

nothing but red-faced, black-haired, rat-fetus smooth beauty
writhing and blindly moving toward the breast?

All these years later and I'm floored by this first freedom,
splayed out on the carpet like a scene from a movie,

a cartoon character flattened by a steam roller
or maybe a teen laid out dizzy from love and drink,

a crime victim with that one unnaturally bent leg.
Only this is me, alone and unaudienced, bowing

to the pine trees and the books on shelves so high
I'll have to climb on furniture to learn how birds behave.

Bowing to the birds. Bowing to my daughter. Bowing to myself,
big bellied as Buddha and just as deserving.

Tishre

Every evening the night forgives the day
and the day sleeps cradled and dreamless,
and every morning the day forgives the night
even its darkest corners of trespass
and the night wanders on dreams of light and wind.

This is the secret of the workings of the world
first seed planted in the primordial deep
first lesson of the Divine when it stepped
out of itself onto the slick, dark lid
of otherness.

Today I crack that seed open with my teeth
heart dividing like dry earth
suddenly seeped through with muddy everything: ocean
and birdsong and things like loss and love that creep,
the world wet and new as in the first days of creation.

Today I forgive the parts of myself that did not grow,
the parts already lain to rest,
I forgive the One who counted to a billion and then forgot to seek
and I forgive my heart its hardest and its softest ways,
wound after wound reveals and I forgive them all

until I feel myself empty at the end of the day, sleek,
held between two lights that love each other well.

Notes

"Flight"
The early story of Lilith in the satirical *Alphabet of Ben Sira* takes a dark turn; I stopped short. Lilith has a long history in many cultures. Here she is identified as the "first woman," created before Eve.

"Taste"
The Talmud brings this teaching in Berachot 40a. Nowhere in the Hebrew Bible or later Jewish commentaries is the fruit of the tree identified as an apple. The rabbis argue (playfully) that it was grapes, wheat, or figs and, elsewhere, a citron. The apple most likely grew from the Latin translation of the bible.

"Naamah"
Noah's wife is not named in the Torah. In rabbinic commentary, she is named Naamah. "Why was she called Naamah? Because she beat her drum (*manemet*) as a form of idol worship (*Midrash Genesis Rabbah* 23)." The midrash makes a sound play from the shared root letters נעם (n'm). In contrast, "Noah was righteous and perfect in his generation. Noah walked with God" (Genesis 6:9).

"Bird Call Koan with Glossary"
Numi numi is a popular Hebrew lullaby. The lyrics are attributed to Yechil Halperin (1880-1942).

"Ciphers and Constellations"
The title is from a painting by Joan Miró: *Ciphers and Constellations in Love with a Woman* (1941).

"*Klippot*"
Shells or husks in Hebrew. It is also a Kabbalistic term, denoting the places that block access to Divine light.

"*Tashlich*"
At the Jewish New Year, this ritual involves tossing breadcrumbs into a natural water source to symbolize casting away sins from the previous year.

"Hamsah"
An ancient amulet rooted in Arabic and Sephardic Jewish cultures, shaped like a hand to symbolize Divine protection.

"*Havdalah*"
From the Hebrew root for separation, the *havdalah* ritual marks the transition from the end of Sabbath to the following week. In one midrash, when night falls, Adam is afraid. God teaches Adam and Eve to make fire and recite the blessing.

"Inside the *Genizah*"
From the Old Persian *ganza* (treasure, hidden), a *genizah* is a repository for discarded, damaged, or defective Jewish texts containing the name of God.

"Sonnet for Habib Koité"
Habib Koité is a Malian guitarist, singer, and songwriter.

"Summoning the *Shechinah*"
In Kabbalistic lore, the *Shechinah*, the feminine aspect of the Divine, comes to dwell among the Jewish people on the Sabbath.

"New Moon of the Month of *Nissan*"
In the Jewish lunar calendar, Passover is celebrated in the month of *Nissan*.

"Desert Is a Mouth Opening"
The Hebrew word for desert, *midbar* (מדבר), makes a sound play with the word *midaber*, to speak.

"*Tishre*"
The first day of the month of *Tishre* marks Rosh Hashanah, the beginning of the Jewish lunar year. Traditionally, this is also the birthday of all of creation.

Acknowledgments

With gratitude to the editors of the following publications in which poems have appeared, some in earlier incarnations:

2River View: "Seventh Day in the Valley"

The Bitter Oleander: "Arterials," "The Desert Is a Mouth Opening," "Entrance to the Letter *Aleph*," "Meridian," "New Moon in the Month of *Nissan*," "Two Dreams at Beth El"

Blue Lyra Review: "*Klippot*," "Naamah"

Bridges: A Jewish Feminist Journal: "Miriam's Skin"

Comet Magazine: "The States that Made Me"

Cottonwood Magazine: "Shooting the Square"

December: "Inside the Room, Outside the Night"

Frontier Poetry: "On Becoming a Woman"

Full: An Anthology of Moon Poems: "Notturno in D"

The Hippocrates Poetry and Medicine Prize Anthology: "Learning the Essentials"

Kerem: "A Woman Asks to Be Named"

Levee Magazine: "The Apple Tree and the Fig Tree"

Lilith Magazine: "7 a.m. at the Wall," "*Tashlich*," "*Tishre*"

Omnium Gatherum Quarterly: "Bird Call Koan with Glossary"

The Raven's Perch: "Hamsah"

Schuylkill Journal of the Arts: "Driving My Mother to Acupuncture"; reprinted in *The Well of Living Water Anthology* and *Gratitudes: To Our Mothers*

The Seattle Review: "All These Gaps"

Slippery Elm Journal: "Safety Matches"

Voices Israel Anthology: "Birdwatcher," "Late Afternoon at Café Roma," "Morning After a Vipassana Retreat," "*Techelet*"

The Well of Living Water Anthology: "A Lesson in Fractions"

Why to These Rocks: 50 Years of Poems from the Community of Writers: "*Yehi Or* (And There was Light)"

Wild Gods: The Ecstatic in Contemporary Poetry and Lyrical Prose: "Inside the *Genizah*," "Rio Caliente"

Wild Roof Journal: "Brown-headed Cowbirds"

Written Here: "Alone on My Daughter's First Night of Sleepaway Camp"

Yentl's Revenge: The Next Wave of Jewish Feminism: "Eve's Confession"

The seeds for this book were planted long ago, and it's a joy to see them bear fruit. I am grateful for my teachers: Chana Bloch z"l, mentor and friend, for her guidance and generosity. Chana Kronfeld, "the other Chana," for tuning my ear to the nuances of text. Elliot Ginsburg and Avivah Zornberg, who awakened my love of Torah study in the 1980s and are still my teachers today. Laura Levitt, Lori Lefkovitz, and Miriam Peskowitz, the brilliant women who inspired me in rabbinical school. Sharon Olds, Brenda Hillman, Lucille Clifton, Galway Kinnell, and all my teachers at the Community of Writers in Olympic Valley. Bob Hass gave me the courage to include a poem that translates bird calls. Gratitude to Brett, Lisa, and the elves.

For my friends: Lisa Wenzel and Jon Riccio for their close readings of this book. Zoom and garden poetry exchanges with Lisa kept me writing through the pandemic. Helisa, Val, Liz, and Emily for their support. My students of all ages, many who grew into friends—Yvonne, Susannah, Nina, and Jacob, to name a few. Thank you to the servers at Solano Junction, Bua Luang Thai, Café Raj, Everest Kitchen, and all my "offices" in my Albany neighborhood.

For my editors: Kim Davis and the staff at Madville Publishing, especially my editor Linda Parsons for her endless patience and astounding precision. Thank you for encouraging me to keep Jewish identity front and center. Paul B. Roth, publisher of *The Bitter Oleander*, for decades-long interest in my work. Danya Ruttenberg selected my essay "You Take Lilith, I'll Take Eve: A Closer Look at the World's Second Feminist" for *Yentl's Revenge: The Next Wave of Jewish Feminism*, which inspired the framework for the book.

Thank you to my parents z"l, who kept a copy of every journal that published my poems. I am sorry you aren't here to celebrate this first book with me. Thank you to those who provided spiritual nourishment from different traditions. Rabbi SaraLeya Schley, Sheppard Powell, Ibrahim Baba z"l—you held me through the birth of my child and the loss of my parents. Thank you most of all to Noam for offering your mad computer skills and engaging in conversations about balancing privacy with the need to use arts to educate and bring about change. Thank you, my math-brained daughter, for putting up with your poet mom. I love you.

These poems were written before October 7, 2023, but these words of gratitude are written after. I first lived in Israel as a kid and have returned many times to study, write, and teach Israeli, Arab, and American youth. I remain connected as a member of Voices Israel, a community of English language poets living in Israel. On October 7, member Judih Weinstein and her husband were fatally wounded by Hamas while taking a walk on their kibbutz. Months later, their bodies remain in Gaza. Their tragic story is one of hundreds from that day; the stories of Palestinian suffering, displacement, and loss loom so large they are still a collective wail. I pray for an end to the cycles of violence and suffering and leave with this fragile haiku by poet Judih Weinstein that appeared in the 2022 Voices Israel anthology:

Oh mother earth
more seeds less destruction
may planters find strength

About the Author

Yiskah Rosenfeld is the author of *Naked Beside Fish* (Finishing Line Press, 2024), an ekphrastic chapbook. She holds an MFA in poetry from Mills College and an MA in jurisprudence and social policy from UC Berkeley. She is also a proud rabbinical school dropout. A Pushcart Prize nominee, she was awarded the Anna Davidson Rosenberg Prize, the Reuben Rose Memorial Prize, and was runner-up for the Jeff Marks Prize, the Julia Darling Prize, and, most recently, the Frontier Poetry Roots & Roads Prize. *Tasting Flight* was the runner-up for the Arthur Smith Poetry Prize and a finalist for the Wheelbarrow Books Poetry Prize. Poems appear in *Lilith Magazine*, *The Seattle Review*, *The Bitter Oleander*, *Rattle*, *Slippery Elm*, *December*, and elsewhere. Her writings have also appeared in anthologies such as *Why to These Rocks: the 50th Anniversary Anthology of the Community of Writers*, *Wild Gods: An Anthology of Ecstatic Poetry*, and *Yentl's Revenge: The Next Wave of Jewish Feminism*. Kansas born and raised, Yiskah currently lives in the San Francisco Bay Area where she balances solo parenting with teaching workshops on feminism, spirituality, and creativity.

www.yiskahrosenfeld.com

www.ingramcontent.com/pod-product-compliance
Lightning Source LLC
Chambersburg PA
CBHW021406090426
42742CB00009B/1035